South Korea Travel Guide 2023

Adventure Awaits: Making the Most of Your Time and Money; Discover the Wonders of South Korea with Insider Tips for Tourists.

Rick Paul

Introduction

I'd always been fascinated by South Korea's rich culture, history, and technology, so when the opportunity arose, I eagerly embarked on a journey to explore the country.

As soon as I arrived in Seoul, I was struck by the city's vibrant energy. Skyscrapers, intricate temples, and bustling street markets captivated me. Every day was full of new experiences, from sampling delectable Korean cuisine to touring historic palaces.

Visiting Jeju Island was one of my most memorable experiences. The breathtaking natural beauty and tranquil landscapes took my breath away, and I was able

to witness the island's traditional culture, including the famous haenyeo female divers.

I realized after two weeks of unforgettable experiences that planning a trip to such a diverse and exciting country could be overwhelming for some. That's why I decided to share my three experiences and insights in order to help others plan their own trip to South Korea.

I put together a detailed itinerary that covers everything from where to stay and what to see to what to eat and how to get around. To make the journey as smooth and enjoyable as possible, I included tips and recommendations based on my own experiences.

It's now your turn. Make use of my itinerary to plan your own unforgettable trip to South Korea. And who knows, maybe you'll be inspired to share your experiences with others one day.

Rick Paul

Contents

Introduction
Welcome to South Korea
    Why travel to South Korea?
    What to do in South Korea
    Tourist Attractions in South Korea
    Festivals And Events In South Korea
    Best Times And Locations To See Cherry Blossom
    The Best Time To Visit For The Seoul Lotus Lantern Festival

Planning Your Trip
    Best time to Visit South Korea
    Budgeting for your trip
    Choosing your itinerary
    Getting to South Korea
    Accommodation options

K-ETA
    A List Of Nations That Have K-ETA
    Exceptions For Submitting An Application For The K-ETA
    K-ETA Application Procedure

Rick Paul

Requirements For The K-ETA
Validity Term
Fees For The K-ETA
Reapplication
Local laws

PLACE TO VISIT: Regions and Destinations
Seoul Province
Busan
Gyeonggi Province
Gangwon Province
Chungcheong Province
Jeolla Province
Gyeongsang Province
Jeju Island
Andong
Incheon and Gyeongin Province

Activities and Experiences
Cultural experiences
Traditional festivals and events
Hiking and Trekking
Beach and Water Sports
Skiing and Snowboarding

Food and Drink Experiences
Traditional Korean cuisine
Street food and snacks
Korean alcohol and tea

Transportation in South korea
The Easiest Form Of Transportation In South Korea
THE KAKAO TAXI
The Usual Method of Paying Kakao Taxi
The Difference Between the Blue and General Taxis
South Korea's KTX Train
Requirements for Obtaining a KTX Train Ticket
The Difference Between a KTX First-Class Ticket and
a Standard-Class Ticket
Process Of Booking A Ferry

Final tips and advice for travelers
Language and Communication
Money and Tipping
Health and Safety
Local Customs and Etiquette
Technology and Connectivity
Future travel considerations

Rick Paul

O<small>NE</small>

Welcome to South Korea

South Korea is a dynamic and culturally rich East Asian country. It has become a popular travel destination in recent years due to its beautiful landscapes, modern cities, and unique cultural experiences. In this guide, we will look at the various reasons why you should visit South Korea in 2023.

South Korea, officially known as the Republic of Korea, is a country located on the Korean Peninsula's southern half. It is bounded to the north by North Korea, to the east by the Sea of Japan, to the west by the Yellow Sea, and to the south by the Korea Strait. The country's history dates back to the Neolithic period, and many ancient temples, palaces, and fortresses still stand today.

South Korea has a population of over 51 million people, with Seoul, the capital city, being the largest city. Busan, Incheon, and Daegu are also important cities. Korean is the official language, and the South Korean won is the currency.

Why travel to South Korea?

South Korea is an excellent travel destination for a variety of reasons. Here are a few examples:

1. Beautiful landscapes

South Korea is known for its stunning landscapes, which range from mountain ranges in the north to beaches in the south. There are 22 national parks in the country, each with its own distinct features and attractions. Seoraksan,

Bukhansan, and Jirisan are among the most popular national parks.

South Korea has many beautiful islands in addition to its national parks. Jeju Island, off the country's southern coast, is a popular tourist destination known for its beaches, waterfalls, and hiking trails.

2. Rich culture and history

South Korea has a rich cultural and historical heritage that is deeply embedded in its society. Many ancient temples, palaces, and fortresses date back hundreds of years in the country.

Gyeongbokgung Palace, located in the heart of Seoul, is one of the most popular historical sites in South Korea. The palace was built in the 14th century and served as the

Joseon dynasty's main royal palace.

South Korea is also well-known for its one-of-a-kind cultural experiences. Visitors can sample traditional Korean cuisine, take part in a tea ceremony, and even learn how to make kimchi, a Korean staple.

3. Modern cities

South Korea is a modern and vibrant country that is steeped in history and tradition. Seoul, in particular, is well-known for its modern architecture, shopping, and entertainment.

Gangnam, a district known for its upscale shopping and nightlife, is one of Seoul's most popular areas. Myeong-dong, a shopping district with over 1,000 stores, and Hongdae, a trendy area known for its street performances and nightlife, are two other popular areas.

4. Technological advancements

South Korea is a technological powerhouse, particularly in the fields of electronics and robotics. Visitors to South Korea can immerse themselves in cutting-edge technology by visiting one of the country's many technology museums and exhibitions.

The Samsung Innovation Museum in Suwon is one of the most popular technology museums in South Korea. The museum exhibits Samsung Electronics' history as well as the company's technological advancements over the years.

5. K-Pop and Korean entertainment

South Korea is well-known for its thriving entertainment industry, particularly in K-Pop music. K-Pop has become a

Rick Paul

global phenomenon in recent years, with fans from all over the world flocking to South Korea to immerse themselves in the music and culture.

Visitors to South Korea can go to concerts and see K-POP.

What to do in South Korea

South Korea has a fascinating history and a rich cultural heritage, which can be seen in the country's historic palaces, temples, and fortifications. Visitors can participate in traditional celebrations such as the Boryeong Mud Festival and the Pusan International Film Festival, as well as learn about the country's unique way of life by visiting its cultural institutions, galleries, and museums.

South Korea has some of the most breathtaking natural vistas on the planet. Visitors can take walks through lush woods, see picturesque mountain ranges, and relax on peaceful beaches. Another reason for the country's fame is its hot springs, which provide a peaceful and refreshing experience.

Attractions of the Present: South Korea, a country with a thriving economy and cutting-edge technology, has a wide range of modern attractions in its major cities. Visitors can explore modern technology, as well as shopping, entertainment, and some of the world's largest amusement parks.

Rick Paul

South Korean cuisine is delicious, savory, and nutritious. Visitors can eat traditional Korean fare such as bibimbap, bulgogi, and kimchi as well as a variety of foreign foods. The country also has a large number of street food stands that offer a unique and delectable eating experience.

Tourist Attractions in South Korea

Historical and Cultural Attractions: South Korea has a diverse range of historical and cultural sites for tourists to explore. The historic city of Gyeongju, Seoul's Gyeongbokgung Palace and the nearby Gwanghwamun Plaza, and Suwon's Hwaseong Fortress are among the most well-known destinations. Visitors can also visit the National Museum of Korea and the National Palace Museum of Korea for more information on South Korean history and culture.

South Korea is rich in natural beauty, with breathtaking

Rick Paul

landscapes, picturesque parks, and scenic coastline regions. Some of Korea's most well-known natural attractions include Jeju Island, Seoraksan National Park, and the Baekdudaegan Mountain Range. Visitors can also visit Namsan Park and Bukhansan National Park to enjoy the lush scenery and abundant foliage.

Adventure Activities: South Korea offers a variety of thrilling activities for those seeking adventure. Visitors can go rafting, hiking, mountain climbing, and enjoy winter activities like skiing and snowboarding. Adventurers can also try bungee jumping, zip lining, and paragliding for a truly thrilling experience.

Shopping and entertainment: South Korea has a wide range of shopping options, from traditional markets to cutting-edge malls. The crowded streets of Seoul's Myeong-dong, the age-old Insadong market, and the massive COEX Mall are all popular shopping destinations. Visitors can also spend the evening at one of the many

entertainment venues, such as theaters, music halls, and movie theaters, or watch a traditional Korean performance, such as a samulnori drumming display.

Festivals And Events In South Korea

Throughout the year, South Korea celebrates a number of national holidays with everything from parades to fireworks. Among the most important holidays are New Year's Day, Independence Day, and National Foundation Day. Visitors should also be aware that Chuseok, or Korean Thanksgiving, and the Lunar New Year, both known as Seollal, are important holidays celebrated in South Korea with family reunions, regional cuisine, and other festivities.

Cultural Festivals: South Korea's numerous cultural festivals serve to highlight the country's rich customs, history, and cultural heritage. Among the most well-known events are the Pusan International Film Festival, the Jinju Namgang Yudeung Festival, and the Boryeong Mud Festival. The Buyeo Seodong Lotus Festival, the Andong International Mask Dance Festival, and the Seoul Lantern Festival are also worth seeing.

Religious Celebrations: Due to South Korea's extensive religious history, visitors can attend a variety of religious events throughout the year. Among the most important events are the Confucian ceremony of Charye, the Catholic procession of the Holy Cross, and the Buddhist lantern festival. Visitors should also see the gut ceremony, which is performed by traditional Korean shamans to honor and seek the blessings of the dead.

Best Times And Locations To See Cherry Blossom

In South Korea, a well-known destination for cherry

blossom viewing, there are several locations that offer breathtaking views of the pink and white flowers. Here are some of the best places and times to see cherry blossoms in South Korea:

Yeouido Park: Yeouido Park is a well-known location in Seoul for cherry blossom viewing. More than 1,000 cherry trees line the banks of the Han River. From late March to early April is the best time to visit. The Jinhae Gunhangje Festival, held in Jinhae on South Korea's southern coast, is famous for its large cherry blossom display, street food vendors, live music, and traditional Korean entertainment. The celebration takes place in early April.

Gyeongju Cherry Blossom Event: This festival, held in Gyeongju, South Korea's southeast, is known for its spectacular display of cherry blossoms around Bomun Lake. The celebration takes place in late April.

Rick Paul

Seokchon Lake: With over 600 cherry trees surrounding the lake, Seokchon Lake is a popular spot for cherry blossom viewing in Seoul. The best time to visit is from late March to early April.

Wolyeonggyo Bridge: This Daegu bridge is well-known for its cherry blossom displays, with over 1,400 cherry trees bordering the banks of the Nakdong River. The best time to visit is from late March to early April. Tourists should check the local weather forecast and cherry blossom bloom status before making travel plans, as the exact date of the blooms may change depending on the local temperature and weather.

In advance: To avoid disappointment during cherry blossom season, plan ahead and reserve lodging, transportation, and activities well in advance. Pay attention to crowded times: The cherry blossom season is also a busy time for local transportation and popular tourist destinations, so tourists should be prepared for

Rick Paul

crowds and plan their itinerary accordingly.

Get up early: Consider waking up early in the morning and visiting before the crowds arrive to enjoy the tranquility and beauty of the cherry blossom blooming. Don't forget to bring your camera; cherry blossom season only happens once a year, so capturing the splendor of the blossoms will help you remember the trip.

Respect the environment: Visitors should be mindful of their environmental impact and show respect for the cherry blossom trees and other natural surroundings by not climbing them, leaving trash behind, or otherwise causing harm to the ecosystem.

These tips may assist tourists in making the most of their time in South Korea watching cherry blossoms and preserving special memories of this lovely time of year.

The Best Time To Visit For The Seoul Lotus Lantern Festival

The Seoul Lotus Lantern Festival is an annual event held in the heart of Seoul, South Korea. The event, which celebrates Buddhist culture, features a vibrant display of lanterns of all sizes and shapes, from simple paper lanterns to massive, ornate structures. Residents and visitors alike attend the festival, which is a great way to learn about South Korea's diverse culture and customs.

The best time to visit the Seoul Lotus Lantern Festival is usually in late April or early May, when the event is in full swing. Throughout the festival, visitors can participate in a variety of events and activities, such as lantern-making workshops, traditional Korean performances, and a lantern procession through Seoul's streets.

Visitors are advised to make travel arrangements for the festival in advance due to its popularity and potential for crowds. It's a good idea to plan your travel and lodging ahead of time, as well as to review the festival calendar for any specific events or activities you might be interested in.

Anyone interested in learning more about South Korea's fascinating customs and history should go to the Seoul Lotus Lantern Festival, which is a unique and colorful celebration of South Korean culture.

Rick Paul

Two

Planning Your Trip

There are many factors to consider when planning a trip to South Korea in 2023, from the best time to visit to the most popular attractions. We'll give you all the information you need to plan your ideal South Korea itinerary in this guide.

Best time to Visit South Korea

Your travel preferences will determine the best time to visit South Korea. Here is a breakdown of the seasons in South Korea:

Spring (March to May): Spring is an excellent time to visit South Korea. The weather is pleasant, and the cherry blossoms are fully bloomed. This is also a popular season for festivals, such as the well-known Jinhae Cherry Blossom Festival.

Summer (June to August): South Korean summers can be hot and humid, with temperatures reaching 30°C. This is an excellent time to visit beaches and coastal areas, as well as to attend music festivals.

Fall (September to November): With mild temperatures and beautiful autumn foliage, fall is another great time to visit South Korea. This is also harvest season, so there will be many food festivals.

Winter (December to February): South Korea's winters can be cold and snowy, with temperatures falling below freezing. However, winter sports and activities such as skiing and snowboarding are popular during this time of year.

Budgeting for your trip

Traveling to South Korea can be an unforgettable experience, but it is critical to plan and budget for your trip accordingly. We'll cover everything you need to know about budgeting for your trip to South Korea in this guide.

Accommodation

Accommodation in South Korea can be pricey, especially if you stay in a major city like Seoul. However, there are several options to suit various budgets.

Hostels and Guesthouses

Hostels and guesthouses are popular budget accommodation options in South Korea. They provide low-cost lodging with shared amenities such as bathrooms and kitchens. Hostels and guesthouses can cost anywhere between KRW 10,000 and KRW 50,000 per night, depending on location and amenities.

Hotels

Hotels in South Korea are typically more expensive than hostels and guesthouses, but they also provide greater privacy and comfort. Hotels can range in price from KRW 50,000 to KRW 200,000 per night, depending on location and level of luxury.

Airbnb

Airbnb is another option for lodging in South Korea, providing a variety of affordable options in various parts of the country. Airbnb rentals can cost anywhere from

Rick Paul

KRW 20,000 to KRW 150,000 per night, depending on location and amenities.

Public Transportation

South Korea's public transportation system is extensive, with buses, subways, and trains. The cost of public transportation is relatively low, with a single subway ride in Seoul costing around KRW 1,250. A T-money card, which is a rechargeable transportation card that can be used on buses, subways, and taxis, can also be purchased.

Taxis

Taxis in South Korea are relatively inexpensive in comparison to other countries, with fares starting around KRW 3,800. Taxis, on the other hand, can be more expensive during peak hours or when traveling a long distance.

Rick Paul

Car Rentals

Renting a car is a good option if you want to explore South Korea's countryside or smaller towns. Depending on the type of car and rental company, rental prices can range from KRW 50,000 to KRW 150,000 per day.

Food and Drink

Food and drink in South Korea can be reasonably priced, particularly if you eat at local restaurants or street food stalls.

Local Restaurants

South Korean restaurants provide a variety of affordable options, including traditional Korean dishes such as bibimbap and bulgogi. A meal at a local restaurant can cost anywhere between KRW 5,000 and KRW 15,000 per person, depending on the restaurant and menu.

Rick Paul

Street Food

Street food is a popular and inexpensive option in South Korea, with a variety of delectable snacks and dishes available. Depending on the vendor and location, street food prices can range from KRW 1,000 to KRW 5,000 per item.

Alcohol

Alcohol is relatively expensive in South Korea, especially if you drink in a bar or club. There are, however, several inexpensive options, such as local beers and soju. A bottle of beer or soju can cost anywhere from KRW 2,000 to KRW 6,000.

Attractions and Activities

From historical sites to modern entertainment, South Korea has something for everyone.

Rick Paul

Historical Sites

South Korea has a long history and numerous historical sites, such as palaces, temples, and museums. Depending on the site and location, admission fees for historical sites can range from KRW 1,000 to KRW 10,000 per person.

Entertainment

South Koreans are well-known for their entertainment industry, which includes K-pop music, dramas, and movies. You can go to concerts and shows, or you can go to entertainment-related attractions such as theme parks and museums. Depending on the type of activity and location, prices for entertainment can range from KRW 10,000 to KRW 50,000 per person.

Outdoor Activities

Hiking, skiing, and water sports are among the many outdoor activities available in South Korea. Outdoor activities can cost anywhere between KRW 20,000 and

Rick Paul

KRW 100,000 per person, depending on the activity and location.

Miscellaneous Expenses

When budgeting for your trip to South Korea, there are a few other expenses to consider.

Visa Fees

You may need a visa to enter South Korea, depending on your nationality. Visa fees can range from KRW 40,000 to KRW 80,000 for a single entry visa.

Travel Insurance

Travel insurance is strongly advised when visiting South Korea. The cost of travel insurance varies according to the

Rick Paul

coverage and provider.

Souvenirs and Shopping

Souvenirs and shopping can add to your expenses, with prices ranging from KRW 5,000 to KRW 50,000 per item for souvenirs and gifts.

Internet and Phone

Internet and phone services are widely available in South Korea, and travelers have several options. Prices for internet and phone services vary by provider and plan, but can range from KRW 10,000 to KRW 50,000 per day.

Overall Budget

Based on the information provided above, a budget traveler can expect to spend between KRW 50,000 and KRW 100,000 per day in South Korea, which includes lodging, transportation, food, and activities. A mid-range

traveler should budget between KRW 100,000 and KRW 200,000 per day, while a luxury traveler should budget more than KRW 200,000 per day.

It's important to note that these are just estimates; your actual costs will vary depending on your travel style, preferences, and itinerary. You can make the most of your trip to South Korea without overspending if you plan and budget carefully.

Choosing your itinerary

Choosing your itinerary for South Korea can be a fun and exciting process, as there are so many places to visit and things to see. It's important to consider your interests, travel style, and budget when deciding on your itinerary. Here are some tips to help you choose the best itinerary for your trip to South Korea:

Consider Your Interests

South Korea provides visitors with a variety of experiences, including historical sites, cultural activities, outdoor adventures, and modern attractions. When planning your itinerary, keep your interests and priorities in mind. Do you want to learn about Korean culture, visit historical sites, or go on an outdoor adventure? You'll have a more fulfilling and enjoyable trip if you plan your itinerary around your interests.

Consider Your Travel Style

Your travel style will also influence your itinerary selection. Do you prefer a fast-paced vacation with lots of activities or a more relaxed vacation with lots of downtime? Do you prefer to stay in one place for an extended period of time, or do you like to move around a lot? When planning your itinerary, keep your travel style in mind and make sure it fits your preferences.

Consider Your Budget

Rick Paul

Your budget will also influence your itinerary selection. Some South Korean destinations and activities are more expensive than others. When planning your itinerary, keep the cost of transportation, lodging, food, and activities in mind, and make sure it fits within your budget.

Consider Your Timeline

Finally, when planning your itinerary, keep your timetable in mind. How long will you be in South Korea? Will you be able to visit multiple places, or will you be limited to one or two? Make sure your itinerary corresponds to your timeline and that you can see and do everything you want in the time you have available.

You can plan the best itinerary for your trip to South Korea by taking into account your interests, travel style, budget, and timeline.

Getting to South Korea

Incheon International Airport (ICN) and Gimpo International Airport (GMP), both located near Seoul, are two of South Korea's international airports. Other major airports include Gimhae International Airport (PUS) in Busan and Jeju International Airport (JJU) (CJU). Korean Air, Asiana Airlines, and Delta Air Lines are just a few of the major airlines that fly to South Korea. If you are flying from North America or Europe, you may need to change planes in another Asian city.

In addition to flying, there are other modes of transportation to South Korea, such as train or ferry. However, these options may not be feasible for the majority of international travelers.

If you're flying to South Korea, book your flights ahead of time to get the best deals. You can compare prices and schedules by checking with different airlines and online

travel agencies.

When you arrive in South Korea, you must clear immigration and customs. You may be asked to show proof of onward travel, such as a return ticket or itinerary, as a foreign visitor. You can take a taxi, bus, or train to your destination once you've cleared immigration and customs. For example, Incheon International Airport has a convenient airport railroad that connects to Seoul and other South Korean destinations.

With numerous flight options and modern transportation infrastructure, getting to South Korea is relatively simple and convenient. It's also worth noting that international ferries connect South Korea with neighboring countries like China, Japan, and Russia. These services, however, may not be as frequent or reliable as flights, and they may not be practical for the majority of international travelers.

Rick Paul

If you want to travel to South Korea by train, you can do so from neighboring countries such as China or Russia. The Trans-Siberian Railway, which runs from Moscow to Beijing via Mongolia and includes a stop in Pyongyang, North Korea, before continuing on to South Korea, is the most popular route. This route, however, is time consuming and may not be the most practical option for most travelers.

Overall, flying to South Korea is the most practical and convenient way for most international travelers to get there. If you have the time and inclination to look into alternative modes of transportation, there are other ways to get to South Korea that can provide a unique and memorable travel experience.

Accommodation options

When planning a trip to South Korea, accommodation is an important factor to consider. Fortunately, there are numerous options to suit all budgets and preferences.

Hotels and Resorts

South Korea has a diverse range of hotels and resorts to suit all budgets and requirements. There are plenty of options to suit every taste, ranging from luxurious five-star hotels to more affordable options. Many of the hotels are in major cities like Seoul and Busan, and they have amenities like swimming pools, fitness centers, and restaurants.

Guesthouses

Guesthouses are a popular choice for low-budget travelers and those seeking a more authentic cultural experience. They are frequently owned and operated by locals and provide a more intimate and personalized experience than larger hotels. Many guesthouses are housed in traditional Korean hanok houses, offering visitors a one-of-a-kind cultural experience.

Hostels

Hostels are another popular choice for low-cost travelers. They provide dormitory-style lodging and frequently have shared facilities such as kitchens and bathrooms. Private rooms are available in many hostels for those who prefer more privacy.

Homestays

Consider a homestay for a truly authentic cultural experience. Homestays are accommodations in which visitors stay in the home of a local family. This is a once-in-a-lifetime opportunity to learn about Korean culture and way of life firsthand. Local travel agencies or online booking platforms are frequently used to arrange homestays.

Hanok Stays

Rick Paul

Hanok stays are becoming increasingly popular among South Korean visitors. These are accommodations in traditional Korean hanok houses that offer visitors a one-of-a-kind cultural experience. Hanok stays frequently provide traditional Korean meals, cultural activities, and traditional Korean clothing to wear while staying.

Whatever your budget or preferences, there is an accommodation option in South Korea to suit you. It's critical to plan ahead of time and book your accommodations to ensure availability, especially during peak travel seasons.

Rick Paul

Rick Paul

THREE

K-ETA

Foreigners who do not have a visa must apply for and receive a K-ETA online before entering the Republic of Korea. They must provide the necessary information online, including their travel itinerary, to do so.

Travel should be done for business, pleasure, to see family, to attend events, or to meet new people (excluding pursuit of profit).

Beginning September 1, 2021, all foreigners entering Korea from countries that do not require or grant visas must complete the K-ETA. (Only within Ireland) Foreign nationals who do not have a K-ETA or a current visa will be denied boarding on a flight to Korea. You do not need a K-ETA if your visa is still valid.

Please keep in mind that the K-ETA website is at k-eta.go.kr. Unofficial websites should be avoided.

A List Of Nations That Have K-ETA

Mexico, Monaco, New Caledonia, Nicaragua, Palau, Saint Kitts-Nevis, Saint Vincent and the Grenadines, Holy See, Albania, Andorra, Barbados, Dominica, Guam, Guyana, and the United States of America This list includes the following countries: Greece, the Netherlands, Denmark, Latvia, Romania, Luxembourg, Lithuania, Belgium,

Bulgaria, Cyprus, Sweden, Spain, Slovakia, Estonia, Austria, Italy, the Czech Republic, Croatia, Portugal, Poland, France, Finland, Hungary, Norway, Switzerland, Liechtenstein, and Iceland are among the countries represented.

Guatemala, Dominican Republic, Bahamas, Brazil, Saint Lucia, Suriname, Haiti, Antigua and Barbuda, Kazakhstan, Qatar, Thailand, Turkey The United Arab Emirates, Bahrain, Oman, Russia, Montenegro, Bosnia and Herzegovina, Serbia, Nauru, Marshall Islands, Fiji, Tuvalu, Australia, Republic of South Africa, Lesotho, Morocco, Mauritius, Botswana, Seychelles, Eswatini, Canada, Argentina, Honduras, Paraguay, Kuwait, Panama, Peru, New Zealand, Grenada, Brunei Darussalam, Saudi Arabia, and Honk

Exceptions For Submitting An Application For The K-ETA

Only those with a UN passport, an ABTC, a USFK military member, an aircraft or ship crew member, a transfer

passenger, or a direct flight to Jeju Island are exempt from submitting a K-ETA application.

As of January 9, 2023, holders of diplomatic or official passports will not be required to submit a K-ETA application.

K-ETA Application Procedure

- You can submit an application at the K-official ETA's website, www.k-eta.go.kr (PC and mobile app). You must submit your K-ETA application at least 72 hours before traveling to the Republic of Korea by ship or plane.
- (Due to an increase in K-ETA applications, the process is currently taking more than 72 hours.)
- A proxy may submit your application on your behalf. Up to 30 people may apply at the same time.

Requirements For The K-ETA

A valid passport, a current profile photo, and an email address are also required.

Check the outcome - Within 72 hours of submitting your application, you can check the outcome via email or online.

(Because of the increased number of K-ETA applications, the process now takes more than 72 hours.)

Validity Term

The validity period begins on the date of approval and lasts two years.

Fees For The K-ETA

The cost is 10,000 KRW ($9-$10). Other fees are not included.

Rick Paul

Reapplication

Please keep in mind that once the application has been submitted, the data entered cannot be changed. Even if your current K-ETA is still valid, you must reapply if you provided incorrect or changed information about your name, gender, date of birth, nationality, passport information (passport number or expiration date), criminal history, and infectious disease information. Those who have a current K-ETA are exempt from filling out the arrival card.

K-ETA IS NOT A VISA, for your information and clarification. K-ETA approval does not guarantee admission to the Republic of Korea; the final decision will be made at the port of entry by a Korea Immigration Service representative. Because the K-ETA center is not in charge of quarantine, please contact the appropriate agency for more information on the requirements. (1339)

Local laws

You can apply for a K-ETA (or visa waiver) for travel to South Korea online. At least 72 hours before departure, the K-ETA application must be submitted. Admission and exit conditions may abruptly change. For the most up-to-date information, contact the South Korean embassy or consulate nearest you.

Unless you are traveling from China, Hong Kong, or Macau, you do not need to take a pre-departure COVID-19 test or a PCR test upon arrival to enter South Korea.

Before boarding their flight to South Korea, passengers departing from China, Hong Kong, or Macau must provide a negative COVID-19 test result. This could be a PCR test performed up to 48 hours before your flight or a supervised RAT test performed up to 24 hours before your flight.

Rick Paul

Every visitor entering South Korea from China, Hong Kong, or Macau must immediately undergo a PCR test and isolate themselves while waiting for the results. Foreign nationals must take the test as soon as possible. Both Korean nationals and long-term residents are eligible to take the exam right away.

If your COVID-19 status is confirmed upon arrival, you must either self-isolate at home or be isolated for 7 days in a government facility if you are a Korean citizen or long-term resident.

Before visiting South Korea, you should register your personal information with the Korean Q-code registration system at the Q-code website. When you arrive, you will be given a QR code that has been generated. Before boarding, passengers from China, Hong Kong, or Macau must register using the Q-code system.

FOUR

PLACE TO VISIT: Regions and Destinations

South Korea is an enthralling country with a rich history, vibrant culture, and breathtaking scenery. It is divided into regions, each with its own set of attractions and destinations. Here is a breakdown of the regions and some of the best places to visit in each.

Seoul Province

Seoul is South Korea's capital and one of Asia's most vibrant and dynamic cities. It is a modern metropolis with a rich cultural heritage that provides visitors with a mix of traditional and modern experiences. The ancient palaces of Gyeongbokgung, Changdeokgung, and Deoksugung, as well as the bustling shopping district of Myeong-dong and the iconic Namsan Tower, are all must-see attractions in Seoul. There is also a thriving food scene in the city, with a wide range of traditional Korean dishes to try.

Neighborhoods and Attractions

Seoul is divided into distinct neighborhoods, each with its own distinct atmosphere and attractions. Some of the best neighborhoods to visit in Seoul are:

Myeong-dong: Myeong-dong is a popular shopping district in Seoul's heart. It's famous for its shops and boutiques, as well as its street food stalls and traditional Korean restaurants. Myeong-top dong's attractions include the Myeong-dong Cathedral, the Namsan Tower, and the Myeong-dong Street Market.

Gangnam: Gangnam is a trendy neighborhood in southern Seoul made famous by the song "Gangnam Style." It is well-known for its upscale shopping, nightlife, and entertainment options, as well as its sleek and contemporary architecture. The COEX Mall, the Gangnam Underground Shopping Center, and the Bongeunsa Temple are among the top attractions in Gangnam.

Hongdae: Hongdae is a popular neighborhood in western Seoul near Hongik University. It's famous for its vibrant nightlife, street performances, and indie music scene. The Hongdae Free Market, the Trick Eye Museum, and the Rolling Hall music venue are among the top attractions in Hongdae.

Insadong: Insadong is a historic district in central Seoul. It

Rick Paul

is well-known for traditional Korean arts and crafts such as ceramics, calligraphy, and folk paintings. The Ssamziegil shopping complex, the Jogyesa Temple, and the Bukchon Hanok Village are among the top attractions in Insadong.

Itaewon: Itaewon is a multicultural district in central Seoul. It is well-known for its international cuisine, nightlife, and shopping opportunities. Itaewon's top attractions include the Itaewon Antique Furniture Street, the National Museum of Korea, and the Korean War Memorial.

Food and Dining Options

Seoul is a foodie's dream, with a wide range of traditional Korean dishes as well as international cuisine options. Among the must-try Korean dishes in Seoul are:

Bibimbap: A popular Korean dish that combines rice, vegetables, and sometimes meat in a spicy gochujang sauce.

Kimchi: Kimchi is a spicy fermented vegetable dish that is commonly served as a side dish in Korean cuisine.

Bulgogi: A Korean barbecue dish that consists of marinated beef or pork grilled over an open flame.

Jjimdak: A spicy Korean chicken and vegetable stew served with noodles.

Tteokbokki: Spicy rice cakes, a popular Seoul street food snack.

Aside from traditional Korean cuisine, Seoul has a wide range of international dining options, including Japanese, Chinese, Italian, and American restaurants. Myeong-dong, Gangnam, and Itaewon are some of Seoul's best dining districts.

Shopping and Markets

Seoul is a shopper's paradise, with everything from high-end luxury brands to trendy street fashion available. The following are some of the best shopping districts in Seoul:

Myeong-dong: This district is well-known for its numerous shops and boutiques, as well as its street food stalls and traditional Korean restaurants.

Dongdaemun: A well-known shopping district known for its numerous wholesale and retail markets, such as the Dongdaemun Fashion Market and the Dongdaemun Design Plaza.

Insadong: A historic district known for traditional Korean arts and crafts such as ceramics, calligraphy, and folk paintings.

Rick Paul

Namdaemun Market: One of Seoul's oldest and largest traditional markets, offering a wide range of goods such as clothing, accessories, and food.

COEX Mall: A massive shopping complex in Gangnam that features a wide range of high-end luxury brands and international chains.

Nightlife and Entertainment

Seoul's nightlife scene is vibrant, with a wide range of entertainment options available, including nightclubs, bars, and live music venues. Some of Seoul's best nightlife and entertainment options include:

Gangnam clubs: Gangnam's high-end clubs and nightlife scene are well-known, with popular venues such as Octagon, Arena, and Ellui.

Hongdae live music: Hongdae is known for its indie music scene, which includes a variety of live music venues and street performances.

Itaewon bars: Itaewon has a lively pub scene as well as a variety of international bars and clubs.

Namsan Tower: Namsan Tower is a popular tourist attraction that provides stunning nighttime views of the city as well as a variety of dining and entertainment options.

Lotte World: Lotte World is a massive indoor amusement park with numerous rides, shows, and attractions, as well as an outdoor Magic Island.

Overall, Seoul provides a diverse range of neighborhoods, attractions, food, shopping, and entertainment options, making it a must-see destination for anyone visiting South Korea.

Rick Paul

Busan

Busan is a bustling port city in South Korea's southeastern region. It is the second-largest city in the country and is known for its beautiful beaches, vibrant nightlife, and diverse culinary scene. Here are some of Busan's highlights:

Beaches and water sports

Busan has some of South Korea's best beaches, making it a popular destination for water sports enthusiasts and beachgoers. With its long stretch of golden sand and clear blue waters, Haeundae Beach is the city's most famous beach. Swimming, jet skiing, parasailing, and other water sports activities are available to visitors. Gwangalli Beach is another popular destination, particularly for its nighttime views of the Gwangan Bridge. Songjeong Beach is a more tranquil option, with a more relaxed atmosphere and excellent surfing opportunities.

Rick Paul

Cultural and historical attractions

Busan has a rich cultural and historical heritage that deserves to be discovered. The Busan Tower, the city's most famous landmark, offers breathtaking panoramic views of the city and the ocean. Another popular attraction is the Beomeosa Temple, which dates back to the 7th century and features beautiful architecture and tranquil surroundings. The Gamcheon Culture Village is a vibrant neighborhood that has recently become a major tourist attraction due to its vibrant murals, art installations, and quirky cafes.

Food and drink options

Busan is known for its diverse culinary scene, which includes both local and international options. The city is well-known for its seafood dishes, and Jagalchi Market is a popular place to try fresh seafood. Other regional delicacies include dwaeji gukbap (riced pork soup),

milmyeon (cold noodle soup), and ssiat hotteok (sweet pancakes with seeds). In addition, visitors can enjoy Korean barbecue, international cuisine, and a variety of street food options.

Shopping and markets

Busan has a diverse shopping scene, ranging from modern shopping malls to traditional markets. Shinsegae Centum City is the world's largest department store and a must-see for any shopper. The Gukje Market is a traditional market that has been in operation for over 60 years, selling a variety of goods such as clothing, accessories, and souvenirs. Nampodong Street, which has a variety of shops, cafes, and street food vendors, is another popular shopping destination.

Gyeonggi Province

Gyeonggi Province, which surrounds Seoul, is home to a

number of popular tourist attractions, including the UNESCO World Heritage site of Suwon Hwaseong Fortress, the Korean Folk Village, and Everland Theme Park.

Neighborhoods and Attractions

Suwon: Suwon is the capital of Gyeonggi Province and is known for its historic sites, including the UNESCO World Heritage Site Hwaseong Fortress. Suwon also has a thriving cultural scene, with museums, galleries, and festivals galore.

Paju: Located near the North Korean border, Paju is home to a number of cultural attractions, including the DMZ Museum, which provides an in-depth look at the Korean War and the ongoing conflict between North and South Korea. Paju also has several art galleries and bookstores.

Gwangmyeong: Gwangmyeong is known for its

underground shopping mall, which is Asia's largest, as well as its unique attractions, such as the Gwangmyeong Cave, a former mine that has been converted into a cultural and recreational space.

Yongin: Yongin is home to several amusement parks, including Everland Resort, one of Asia's largest theme parks, and Caribbean Bay, a water park that is part of the same resort.

Food and Dining Options

Gyeonggi Province is well-known for its traditional Korean cuisine, which includes a wide range of rice, vegetable, meat, and seafood dishes. The following are some popular dishes to try in Gyeonggi Province:

Galbi: Galbi is a Korean-style grilled beef or pork dish marinated in a sweet and savory sauce.

Rick Paul

Bibimbap: Bibimbap is a rice bowl dish that is often served with gochujang sauce and is topped with a variety of vegetables, meat, and a fried egg.

Japchae: Japchae is a stir-fried noodle dish made with sweet potato noodles and various vegetables and meat.

Samgyetang: Samgyetang is a traditional Korean soup made with chicken, ginseng, and other ingredients that is thought to have medicinal properties.

Shopping and Markets

Gyeonggi Province has a wide range of shopping and market opportunities, including:

Ilsan Lake Park: Ilsan Lake Park is a popular shopping and entertainment complex with a wide range of stores, restaurants, and cultural attractions.

Munjeong-dong Rodeo Street: Munjeong-dong Rodeo Street is a trendy shopping district with a wide range of clothing and accessory stores, as well as restaurants and cafes.

Yangjae Flower Market: Yangjae Flower Market is South Korea's largest flower market, offering a wide variety of flowers, plants, and gardening supplies.

Nightlife and Entertainment

While Gyeonggi Province is not known for its nightlife, there are still plenty of options for entertainment, including:

Everland Resort: During the summer months, Everland Resort offers a variety of rides, shows, and attractions, as

well as a nightly fireworks show.

Icheon Ceramics Village: Icheon Ceramics Village is a traditional Korean pottery village that offers a variety of workshops, exhibits, and cultural activities.

Gyeonggi Arts Center: The Gyeonggi Arts Center is a cultural complex that hosts exhibitions, performances, and workshops in the fields of music, dance, and visual arts. The center is in Suwon and is easily reached by public transportation. It has a modern and spacious design and is an excellent place to learn about Korean culture and art.

Throughout the year, the center hosts a variety of events, including concerts, theater performances, dance shows, and exhibitions of contemporary and traditional art. Regular workshops and classes are also available for those interested in learning about Korean arts and culture.

The Gyeonggi International Ceramic Biennale, which is held every two years and attracts artists and art enthusiasts from all over the world, is one of the most popular events held at the Gyeonggi Arts Center. The biennale includes sculptures, installations, and functional objects in addition to ceramic artworks.

The Gyeonggi Arts Center includes a library, a cafe, and a gift shop where visitors can purchase souvenirs and artwork, in addition to the main performance and exhibition spaces. The center is an excellent place to spend an afternoon or evening learning about Korean arts and culture.

Gangwon Province

Gangwon Province is known for its beautiful natural landscapes and is located in the northeast of South Korea. It is home to several national parks, including Seoraksan National Park, one of the country's most popular hiking destinations. The ski resorts of Pyeongchang and Gangneung, which hosted the Winter Olympics in 2018, are also popular attractions in Gangwon Province.

Neighborhoods and attractions

Pyeongchang: Pyeongchang is a popular winter sports destination that hosted the 2018 Winter Olympics. It provides visitors with a variety of activities such as skiing, snowboarding, and sledding. In the summer, the area is also ideal for hiking and exploring the region's natural beauty.

Gangneung: Gangneung is a coastal city with a long cultural history. It is home to several significant historical sites, including the Gangneung Danoje Festival, which has been designated as a UNESCO Intangible Cultural Heritage of Humanity. Beautiful beaches, hiking trails, and traditional Korean architecture are also available in the city.

Rick Paul

Seoraksan National Park: Hikers and nature enthusiasts flock to Seoraksan National Park. It has breathtaking mountain scenery, waterfalls, and wildlife. There are several hiking trails of varying difficulty in the park, as well as hot springs and Buddhist temples.

Food and dining options

Gangwon-style dakgalbi: Dakgalbi is a spicy stir-fried chicken dish from Gangwon Province. It is a popular dish among both locals and visitors, and is typically served with rice cakes and vegetables.

Pyeongchang-style trout: Trout is a popular fish in Gangwon Province, and this dish is a must-try. The fish is grilled and served with a variety of side dishes, including a sweet and savory sauce.

Rick Paul

Gangneung-style coffee: Gangneung is well-known for its coffee culture, with several popular cafes. Coffee lovers should try the city's coffee, which is made with locally sourced beans.

Shopping and markets

Pyeongchang Trout Festival Market: Every winter, the Pyeongchang Trout Festival allows visitors to catch and grill their own trout. The festival also includes a market where visitors can buy local goods such as handmade crafts and souvenirs.

Gangneung Jungang Market: Gangneung Jungang Market is one of Korea's oldest markets, offering a diverse range of goods such as fresh seafood, vegetables, and traditional Korean snacks.

Nightlife and entertainment

Rick Paul

Yongpyong Resort: Yongpyong Resort is one of Korea's largest ski resorts, offering a variety of winter activities such as skiing, snowboarding, and snowmobiling. Visitors can also enjoy a variety of restaurants, bars, and cafes at the resort.

Gangneung Ice Arena: Built for the 2018 Winter Olympics, the Gangneung Ice Arena is now open to the public. Ice skating and other winter sports, as well as concerts and other events, are available to visitors at the arena.

Chungcheong Province

Chungcheong Province, in the heart of South Korea, is known for its traditional culture and breathtaking natural scenery. Daejeon, known for its science and technology museums, and Gongju, home to several UNESCO World Heritage sites, including the royal tombs of the Baekje Kingdom, are two of the province's top destinations. Here are some of Chungcheong Province's highlights:

Historical and cultural attractions

Chungcheong Province is home to a number of historical and cultural sites that provide a glimpse into Korea's past. The Gongju National Museum, which houses artifacts from the Baekje Dynasty, is one of the most popular attractions. Other notable sites include the Jeonju Hanok Village, a traditional Korean village that showcases Joseon Dynasty architecture and way of life, and the Chungjuho Lake Cultural Center, which showcases Chungju Lake's local history and culture.

Food and drink options

Chungcheong Province is well-known for its delectable cuisine, which is distinguished by its bold and hearty flavors. Chungcheong-do style bibimbap, a rice dish mixed with a variety of vegetables, meat, and chili paste, is one of the region's most famous dishes. Dakgalbi, a spicy chicken

dish cooked on a griddle with vegetables and rice cake, is another local specialty, as is makgeolli, a type of traditional Korean rice wine brewed in the region.

Accommodation options

Accommodation options in Chungcheong Province include traditional Korean hanok houses, guesthouses, and hotels. Many of the hanok houses have been converted into guesthouses, offering visitors a one-of-a-kind cultural experience. Visitors can also stay in a traditional Korean house converted into a museum or cultural center, such as the Gongju National Museum or the Jeonju Hanok Village. There are several hotels and resorts in the province's major cities, including Daejeon and Cheongju, for those seeking a more modern experience.

Jeolla Province

Jeolla Province is located in southwest South Korea and is known for its delicious food and beautiful scenery. The historic city of Jeonju, known for its traditional hanok houses and delicious bibimbap, and the coastal city of Mokpo, a popular destination for seafood lovers, are two of the province's top destinations. Here are some of Jeolla Province's highlights:

Historical and cultural attractions

Several historical and cultural attractions in Jeolla Province provide a glimpse into Korea's past. One of the most well-known attractions is the Jeonju Hanok Village, a traditional Korean village that showcases Joseon Dynasty architecture and way of life. The Gyeonggijeon Shrine, a beautiful shrine that houses the portrait of King Taejo, the founder of the Joseon Dynasty, is also open to visitors. Suncheon Bay Ecological Park, which is home to a diverse array of wildlife, and the Boseong Green Tea Fields, which offer stunning views of the rolling green hills and tea plantations, are two other notable sites.

Food and drink options

Rick Paul

Jeolla Province is well-known for its delectable cuisine, which includes seafood, vegetables, and traditional Korean flavors. Jeonju bibimbap, a rice dish with a variety of vegetables, meat, and chili paste, is one of the region's most famous dishes. Other regional specialties include raw octopus, grilled eel, and sashimi, as well as traditional Korean alcoholic beverages like makgeolli and soju.

Accommodation options

Accommodation options in Jeolla Province include traditional Korean hanok houses, guesthouses, and hotels. Visitors to the Jeonju Hanok Village can stay in a traditional Korean house that has been converted into a museum or cultural center. There are several hotels and resorts in the province's major cities, including Jeonju and Gwangju, for those seeking a more modern experience. In addition, camping and glamping facilities can be found in scenic areas such as Suncheon Bay and Jirisan National

Rick Paul

Park.

Gyeongsang Province

Gyeongsang Province, in the southeast of South Korea, is home to a number of historic and cultural sites. The ancient city of Gyeongju, which was the capital of the Silla Kingdom and is home to several UNESCO World Heritage sites, including the Bulguksa Temple and Seokguram Grotto, is one of the province's top destinations. Busan, which is also in Gyeongsang Province, is known for its beautiful beaches, seafood markets, and stunning temples.

Historical and cultural attractions

Bulguksa Temple: This UNESCO World Heritage site in Gyeongju is one of the most important Buddhist temples in South Korea. It was constructed during the Silla Dynasty in the eighth century and features beautiful architecture and artwork.

Rick Paul

Gyeongju Historic Areas: Gyeongju was the Silla Dynasty's capital and is home to numerous historic sites, including the Silla Dynasty Royal Tombs, Cheomseongdae Observatory, and Anapji Pond.

Busan Tower: This iconic Busan landmark offers breathtaking views of the city and the coastline.

Tongyeong Historic Areas: Several historic sites can be found in this coastal city, including the Tongyeong Traditional Fish Market and Dongpirang Village, a colorful hillside village filled with street art.

Food and drink options

Ssiat Hotteok: A sweet pancake filled with seeds and nuts, ssiat hotteok is a popular street food in Gyeongsang

Province.

Deodeok Gui: A regional specialty made with grilled deodeok, a type of mountain herb.

Haejangguk: This spicy soup made of beef, pork, and vegetables is said to be an excellent hangover remedy.

Makgeolli: A popular drink in Gyeongsang Province, this traditional rice wine is often served with savory pancakes or seafood.

Accommodation options

Hanok Guesthouses: Stay in a traditional Korean house at one of Gyeongsang Province's many hanok guest houses, such as the Bomun Hanok Village in Gyeongju.

Beach Resorts: Beach resorts dot the coastline of Gyeongsang Province, including the Hilton Busan and the Paradise Hotel and Casino in Busan.

Luxury Hotels: Consider the Park Hyatt Busan or the Lotte Hotel Busan for a more upscale stay, both of which

offer stunning views and first-rate amenities.

Jeju Island

Jeju Island is a volcanic island off South Korea's southern coast. It is a well-known tourist destination for its breathtaking natural scenery, which includes waterfalls, beaches, and hiking trails. Some of the top attractions on Jeju Island include the UNESCO World Heritage site Seongsan Ilchulbong Peak and the Jeju Folk Village, which provides a glimpse into traditional Jeju Island life. Here are some of Jeju Island's highlights:

Natural attractions

There are several natural wonders on Jeju Island that are worth exploring. The UNESCO World Heritage-listed Jeju Volcanic Island and Lava Tubes, with dramatic volcanic landscapes, lava tubes, and stunning coastal views, is a must-see. Hallasan National Park is another popular attraction, with hiking trails leading to the summit of Hallasan Mountain, South Korea's highest peak.

Rick Paul

Cheonjiyeon Waterfall, Seongsan Ilchulbong Peak, and Udo Island are among the other natural wonders.

Outdoor activities

Jeju Island is a haven for outdoor enthusiasts, with a plethora of activities to choose from. Hiking is a popular outdoor activity, with trails ranging in difficulty. Water sports such as swimming, surfing, and scuba diving are also popular among visitors, with some of the best spots located near Seogwipo and Jungmun. Horseback riding, cycling, and golf are other popular activities.

Food and drink options

Jeju Island is well-known for its distinctive cuisine, which emphasizes locally sourced ingredients and traditional dishes. Black pork, a type of pork raised on the island and known for its tenderness and flavor, is one of the island's most famous dishes. Other regional specialties include grilled squid, abalone porridge, and grilled mackerel. Visitors should also try Jeju tangerines, hallabong oranges, and green tea, which are popular local products.

Rick Paul

Accommodation options

Jeju Island has a variety of lodging options to suit all budgets and preferences. There are luxury resorts, beachfront hotels, guesthouses, and homestays for visitors to choose from. Jungmun Resort is a popular choice for those seeking a luxurious experience, while Seogwipo provides a variety of mid-range and budget options. There are also some unusual lodging options, such as traditional hanok houses and camping grounds.

Andong

Andong is a city in South Korea's southeastern region known for its rich cultural heritage and historical attractions. Here are some of the top attractions in Andong, as well as some popular food and drink options and lodging options.

Historical and Cultural Attractions

Andong Hahoe Folk Village: This UNESCO World Heritage Site showcases traditional Korean architecture and culture. Visitors can stroll through the village and watch demonstrations of traditional crafts as well as performances of traditional music and dance.

Andong Confucian School: During the Joseon Dynasty, this historical site served as a Confucian academy. Visitors can see traditional Korean architecture and learn about Confucianism.

Bongjeongsa Temple: Located in the Taebaek Mountains' foothills, this temple is known for its beautiful architecture and natural surroundings.

Dosan Seowon: Dosan Seowon is a Confucian academy and shrine founded during the Joseon Dynasty. It is surrounded by stunning natural scenery and provides an insight into traditional Korean culture.

Food and Drink Options

Andong Jjimdak: A local specialty consisting of chicken,

vegetables, and glass noodles cooked in a soy sauce-based broth. It is a popular dish among both locals and visitors.

Heotjesabap: A traditional rice dish made with five different grains that is frequently served with a variety of side dishes.

Andong Soju: A popular drink in Andong, this is a traditional Korean liquor made from rice.

Accommodation Options

Traditional Hanok Guesthouses: There are several traditional hanok guesthouses in Andong where visitors can stay and learn about traditional Korean architecture and culture. Hahoe Hanok Stay and Andong Hanok Village Guesthouse are two popular choices.

Hotels: Andong has a number of hotels to suit a variety of budgets and preferences, including the Andong Grand Hotel and the Andong Park Hotel.

Hostels and Guesthouses: Andong has a number of hostels and guesthouses for budget travelers, including Andong

Goodstay and Andong Poong-Gyung Guesthouse. These provide inexpensive lodging with shared facilities.

Incheon and Gyeongin Province

Incheon is a port city in northwest South Korea that serves as a gateway to the country for many international visitors. It is home to Incheon International Airport, which is one of Asia's busiest. Gyeongin Province, which surrounds Incheon, is known for its cultural attractions, such as the historic city of Paju, which is home to several traditional Korean villages, and the DMZ (Demilitarized Zone) that divides North and South Korea. Several theme parks, including Lotte World and Everland, are also located in the province.

FIVE

Activities and Experiences

Cultural experiences

South Korea has a plethora of cultural experiences to offer visitors, ranging from ancient traditions to modern-day innovations. There are numerous opportunities to learn about Korea's history and customs, to immerse yourself in traditional arts and crafts, or simply to enjoy the vibrant contemporary culture.

Rick Paul

Participating in traditional activities such as tea ceremonies, calligraphy, and hanbok (traditional Korean clothing) dressing is one of the best ways to experience Korean culture. Many museums and cultural centers offer workshops and classes to help you learn these skills and gain a better understanding of Korean culture.

Visitors can also attend traditional festivals and events held throughout the country throughout the year. These festivals provide a glimpse into Korea's rich and diverse cultural traditions, such as food, music, dance, and costumes. Among the most popular festivals in South Korea are:

Boryeong Mud Festival: This festival, held in July in the coastal city of Boryeong, celebrates the healing properties of the city's mineral-rich mud. Mud wrestling, mud slides, and other mud-based activities, as well as live music and fireworks, are available to visitors.

Jinju Lantern Festival: This festival, held in October in Jinju, features hundreds of traditional lanterns of various shapes and sizes. Lantern-making workshops, traditional Korean music and dance performances, and a lantern parade down the Nam River are all available to visitors.

Andong Mask Dance Festival: Held in September in Andong, this festival features traditional Korean mask dances performed to ward off evil spirits and bring good luck. Visitors can observe the performances, try on masks and costumes, and take part in traditional Korean games and activities.

Visitors can attend cultural performances such as traditional Korean music and dance shows in addition to festivals. Among the most popular performances are:

Nanta: This high-energy percussion show combines traditional Korean rhythms with modern beats in a

nonverbal performance. A talented cast of performers uses kitchen utensils as instruments in the show.

Jeongdong Theater: This theater, located in the heart of Seoul, is known for its performances of traditional Korean dance and music. The productions of the theater frequently incorporate elements of modern dance and theater, creating a unique and innovative experience.

Pansori: Pansori is a traditional form of Korean musical storytelling that has been passed down through generations. The solo singer is accompanied by a drummer in the performances, which tell stories of love, tragedy, and heroism.

Overall, South Korea provides visitors with a wealth of cultural experiences to explore, ranging from ancient traditions to modern innovations. There's something for everyone, whether you want to go to festivals, try

traditional activities, or watch cultural performances.

Traditional festivals and events

South Korea is well-known for its vibrant and distinctive traditional festivals and events that honor the country's rich culture and history. Throughout the year, there is always something exciting and fascinating to experience, from colorful parades to elaborate performances and traditional games. Here are some of South Korea's most popular traditional festivals and events:

Lunar New Year (Seollal): Seollal is one of South Korea's most important traditional holidays, celebrated on the first day of the lunar calendar. It is a time for families to gather and pay respect to their ancestors, and it usually occurs in late January or early February. Making and eating rice cakes, playing traditional games, and performing ancestral rites are all traditional customs.

Buddha's Birthday (Seokga Tansinil): Buddha's Birthday, celebrated in May, is one of South Korea's most colorful and vibrant traditional festivals. Temples across the country are festooned with lanterns and colorful decorations, and major cities host parades featuring traditional music and dance.

Dano Festival: Dano Festival is a time for people to pray for good health and fortune. It is held on the fifth day of the fifth lunar month (usually in late May or early June). Swinging on tree branch swings, making traditional rice cakes, and performing traditional Korean folk dances are all traditional activities.

Boryeong Mud Festival: The Boryeong Mud Festival takes place in July in Boryeong and attracts thousands of visitors from all over the world. Mud wrestling, mud sliding, and mud painting are among the fun mud-related activities at the festival.

Andong Mask Dance Festival: The Andong Mask Dance Festival is one of South Korea's largest traditional festivals, held in the city of Andong in October. The festival includes mask dances, traditional music performances, and a traditional market, among other traditional performances and cultural activities.

Chuseok: Another major traditional holiday in South Korea, Chuseok is observed on the 15th day of the eighth lunar month (usually in September or October). Chuseok, like Seollal, is a time for families to gather and pay respect to their ancestors. Making and eating traditional foods, playing traditional games, and performing ancestral rites are all examples of traditional activities.

Seoul Lantern Festival: The Seoul Lantern Festival, held

in November, is a magical event that displays thousands of beautifully lit lanterns throughout the city. The lanterns, which represent various themes and motifs, are designed and created by both local and international artists.

These traditional festivals and events are a fantastic way to immerse yourself in South Korea's rich culture and history. Visitors are encouraged to take part in the various activities and soak up the vibrant atmosphere of these festivals.

Hiking and Trekking

South Korea has numerous hiking and trekking opportunities, ranging from easy walks to difficult climbs. Seoraksan National Park, one of the most popular hiking destinations, offers stunning mountain views and a variety of trails for hikers of all skill levels. Jirisan National Park, which has the highest peak on mainland South Korea and a variety of hiking trails that take you through beautiful forests and mountains, is another popular destination.

There are many other hiking trails scattered throughout the country, in addition to national parks, such as the Bukhansan National Park in Seoul, which offers a variety of trails with stunning views of the city. The Jeju Olle Trail on Jeju Island, with 26 different routes that take you along the island's beautiful coastlines and through small villages, is also a popular choice.

Beach and Water Sports

South Korea has more than 2,000 kilometers of coastline, which provides numerous opportunities for beach and water sports. Some of the most popular beaches are Haeundae Beach in Busan, Gyeongpo Beach in Gangneung, and Jungmun Beach on Jeju Island.

Surfing is becoming more popular in South Korea, with the waves on the east coast being especially welcoming to beginners. Windsurfing and kitesurfing are also popular on Muuido Island near Incheon.

Kayaking, stand-up paddleboarding, and fishing are also popular water sports. Kayaking is particularly popular on Jeju Island, where you can paddle through caves and along the beautiful coastline.

Skiing and Snowboarding

During the winter, South Korea is a popular destination for skiing and snowboarding. Yongpyong Resort in Pyeongchang, which hosted the 2018 Winter Olympics, is the country's largest ski resort. Alpensia Resort in Pyeongchang and High1 Resort in Jeongseon are two other popular ski resorts.

Food and Drink Experiences

South Korean cuisine is well-known, and there are numerous food and beverage experiences to be had throughout the country. Attending a traditional Korean cooking class, going on a street food tour, or visiting a traditional Korean tea house are all popular options.

In Seoul, you can try a variety of street food and local specialties at Gwangjang Market, one of the city's oldest and largest traditional markets. Jeonju, which is known for its traditional Korean cuisine and has a large number of restaurants serving local dishes, is another popular food destination.

There are many tea houses throughout the country that offer tea tastings and traditional tea ceremonies for those interested in traditional Korean tea. The Korean Tea Culture Park in Boseong and the Seokparang Tea Museum on Jeju Island are two popular tea houses.

Overall, South Korea provides a diverse range of outdoor activities and experiences, making it an ideal destination for those who enjoy getting out and exploring. There's something for everyone, whether you want to hike through beautiful mountains, go water skiing on the beach, or eat delicious Korean food.

Traditional Korean cuisine

Traditional Korean cuisine should not be missed by any foodie visiting South Korea. Korean food has grown in popularity in recent years, thanks to its spicy, savory, and fermented flavors. Among the most popular Korean dishes are:

Kimchi: A fermented vegetable dish made with a variety of ingredients such as cabbage, radish, and cucumber, kimchi is a staple in Korean cuisine. It is commonly served

as a side dish and is thought to have numerous health benefits.

Bulgogi: Bulgogi is a popular Korean grilled meat dish made with marinated beef, chicken, or pork. It's usually served with rice and vegetables and has a sweet and savory flavor.

Bibimbap: A rice bowl dish consisting of rice, sautéed vegetables, and meat, topped with a fried egg and spicy sauce. It is a popular option for a nutritious and filling meal.

Jjajangmyeon: Jjajangmyeon is a Korean-Chinese noodle dish that consists of thick wheat noodles, black bean sauce, and vegetables. It's a popular comfort food dish that's usually accompanied by pickled radish.

Rick Paul

Samgyeopsal: Samgyeopsal is a popular Korean pork belly dish that is grilled at the table and served with lettuce leaves, garlic, and a variety of dipping sauces. It's a popular option for a memorable and interactive dining experience.

Street food and snacks

South Korea is also known for its street food and snacks, which are available in markets and food stalls across the country. The following are some popular street food and snack options:

Tteokbokki: Tteokbokki is a popular Korean street food that consists of spicy rice cakes and a sweet and spicy sauce. It's usually accompanied by fish cakes and boiled eggs.

Hotteok: A sweet and chewy Korean pancake stuffed with cinnamon, brown sugar, and chopped nuts. It's a

Rick Paul

popular winter snack that's usually sold by street vendors.

Bungeoppang: Bungeoppang is a fish-shaped pastry filled with sweet red bean paste. It's a popular winter snack that's usually sold by street vendors.

Odeng: Odeng is a skewer of Korean fish cake that is typically boiled in a flavorful broth and served with a dipping sauce. It is a popular winter snack available in markets and food stalls across the country.

Mandu: Mandu is a Korean dumpling that can be boiled, steamed, or fried and is typically filled with meat and vegetables. It is a popular snack available in markets and food stalls across the country.

Korean alcohol and tea

Korean alcohol and tea are also popular options for those looking to sample local beverages. Popular Korean alcoholic beverages include:

Soju: Soju is a clear distilled liquor derived from rice, wheat, or barley. It is the most popular alcoholic beverage in South Korea and is frequently consumed with meals.

Makgeolli: Makgeolli is a milky rice wine traditionally served in a bowl or small pot. It has a slightly sweet and sour taste and is a popular social drink.

Bokbunja ju: Bokbunja ju is a sweet and fruity wine made from black raspberries. It is a popular drink in South Korea and is thought to have a variety of health benefits.

SIX

Transportation in South korea

Air travel: South Korea's two largest international airports, Incheon International Airport and Gimpo International Airport, serve as hubs for both domestic and international flights. Travelers can reach several tourist attractions in South Korea quickly and comfortably by flying to major cities within the country.

Rail Transportation: South Korea's rail network is

Rick Paul

extensive and functional, providing tourists with a convenient and cost-effective mode of transportation. The KTX, the nation's high-speed rail system, connects the major cities and provides a quick and convenient means of long-distance travel. Regional trains and subways are also available, providing fast access to tourist attractions in metropolitan areas.

Road Travel: Visitors who wish to drive in South Korea may do so and enjoy the freedom to explore the country at their own pace. Although the country has a vast network of highways and roads, traffic in major cities can be heavy, so travelers should expect slower speeds.

Local Transportation: South Korea's local transportation network is well developed, consisting of buses, subways, and taxis. Buses are widely available and provide a convenient and cost-effective way to explore both urban and rural areas. Subways, particularly in metropolitan areas, are quick and convenient, whereas cabs are widely

Rick Paul

available and provide a flexible mode of transportation.

Driving in South Korea: Visitors who intend to drive in South Korea should be aware of the country's driving laws and practices. Driving is done on the right side of the road, and everyone in the vehicle must wear a seatbelt. Visitors should also become familiar with traffic signs and be prepared for heavy traffic in metropolitan areas. To drive in South Korea, you must have an international driving permit.

The Easiest Form Of Transportation In South Korea

The most convenient mode of transportation in South Korea is determined by the traveler's preferences, budget, and final destination. However, it is widely agreed that the following options are the most practical:

Subway: South Korea's extensive, quick, and reasonably

priced subway system. It is regarded as one of the best in the world, with coverage of major cities such as Seoul, Busan, and Incheon.

Taxi: For shorter journeys, taxis are a convenient and widely available option in South Korea. They can be hailed on the street or at a taxi stand, and their rates are very reasonable.

THE KAKAO TAXI

Kakao Taxi is a taxi-hailing service in South Korea that uses the Kakao app. The app connects customers with authorized taxi drivers and provides real-time information on the location and condition of accessible cabs. Kakao Taxi has the following features:

The Kakao app makes booking a cab simple by allowing users to enter their pick-up and drop-off locations.

Real-time information: By providing real-time information on the location and status of available taxis, the app allows users to track the progress of their journey.

Kakao Taxi accepts cash, credit/debit cards, and other payment methods.

The app provides information about the driver to promote passenger safety and trust. This data includes the driver's name, photo, and rating.

Customer service: Kakao Taxi offers 24-hour customer service to help with any questions or concerns.

The Usual Method of Paying Kakao Taxi

Credit or debit cards processed through the Kakao app are the standard form of payment for Kakao Taxi in South

Rick Paul

Korea. Following the completion of the trip, the fare is immediately charged to the saved card, and the user receives an email receipt.

Cash, Kakao Pay, and mobile banking apps are just a few of the other payment options offered by Kakao Taxi. Before scheduling a ride, users can select their preferred payment method through the app.

Kakao Taxi is popular in South Korea and is known for providing dependable, quick, and convenient service. It is a popular alternative to traditional taxi services and a convenient option for people who prefer to reserve and pay for their trips using a smartphone app.

The Difference Between the Blue and General Taxis

In South Korea, there are primarily two types of taxis: blue

taxis and regular taxis. The following are the main differences between them:

Blue taxis frequently have a higher base cost and a lower per-kilometer fee than regular taxis. They may be less expensive for longer excursions, but they are frequently more expensive for shorter ones.

Blue taxis are only permitted in major cities; they are not permitted to pick up customers in rural areas. General taxis, on the other hand, can pick up passengers in both urban and rural settings.

Blue taxis frequently feature more modern, higher-end vehicle types, as well as conveniences such as GPS and credit card readers. General taxis may be older vehicles with fewer amenities.

Rick Paul

Driver education: Blue cab drivers must receive additional training and adhere to stricter requirements than regular taxi drivers.

Customer service: Blue taxis are well-known for their excellent customer service and are frequently regarded as more dependable and trustworthy than regular taxis.

While regular taxis can be booked over the phone or through ride-hailing apps like Kakao Taxi, blue taxis can only be hailed from the street.

Blue taxis are frequently delivered faster than regular taxis, resulting in a shorter waiting period.

Blue taxis are a better option for those with a lot of luggage because they often have more luggage space than regular taxis.

GPS and navigation systems are available in blue taxis, which may be useful for customers unfamiliar with the area. These characteristics may not be found in standard taxis.

Comfort: When compared to regular taxis, blue taxis frequently provide a higher level of comfort, such as larger and more comfortable seats, superior air conditioning, and other amenities.

Finally, whether a person chooses a blue taxi or a regular cab is determined by their needs and preferences. While regular taxis are more accessible and may be more cost-effective for shorter journeys, blue taxis provide better service and cars but are frequently more expensive.

Bus: Another convenient mode of transportation within South Korea, especially for longer distances, is the bus.

Rick Paul

They serve both urban and rural areas and are a more affordable alternative to trains and taxis.

South Korea's KTX Train

The Korean State Railway operates South Korea's high-speed KTX (Korea Train Express) railway system. It opened in 2004 and connects Busan, Daejeon, Gwangju, and other major South Korean cities to Seoul, the country's capital. Here are some of the main characteristics of the KTX train:

Speed: With top speeds of 300 km/h, the KTX trains are among the fastest in the world.

Routes: The KTX operates several major lines, including the Gyeongbu Line, Honam Line, and Jeolla Line. Trains leave Seoul Station several times an hour for various destinations, and they run on a regular basis.

Convenience: The KTX trains are outfitted with modern amenities such as air conditioning, comfortable seats, and food and beverage services.

KTX trains are a convenient way to travel between cities because they allow passengers to avoid traffic and arrive at their destinations faster.

In general, both residents and visitors in South Korea regard the KTX as a dependable and efficient mode of transportation.

Requirements for Obtaining a KTX Train Ticket

To purchase a ticket for the South Korean KTX train, the following basic conditions must be met:

Identification: To purchase a ticket, you must present a valid, government-issued picture ID, such as a passport or national ID card.

Cash, credit or debit cards, and KTX tickets are accepted

Rick Paul

forms of payment. Standard-class and first-class KTX tickets are two of the many ticket classes available. You may select the ticket type that best meets your needs and financial situation.

Reservation of a seat: You can reserve a seat in person or online. If you don't have a reservation, you can still buy a ticket and take any open seat.

Stations of departure and arrival: Be sure to indicate the stations of departure and arrival when purchasing your ticket.

Date and time of travel: You must also provide the date and time of your trip. It is best to reserve your KTX ticket in advance to ensure availability, especially during peak travel times. Keep in mind that ticket prices can vary depending on the day and season.

Rick Paul

The Difference Between a KTX First-Class Ticket and a Standard-Class Ticket

In South Korea, the primary distinctions between first-class and regular-class KTX tickets are as follows:

Comfort: First-class seating is more spacious and pleasant than economy seating, with larger seats, more legroom, and more reclining options.

Price: First-class tickets are frequently more expensive than other classes of tickets. There may be a price difference depending on the route and time of travel. First-class passengers frequently receive additional benefits, such as complimentary food and beverages and access to VIP lounges at specific stations.

Privacy: When compared to regular class, first class cabins often have fewer seats per row and offer more privacy.

First-class tickets may be difficult to obtain and may sell

Rick Paul

out quickly, especially during peak travel periods.

Finally, if comfort and privacy are important to you and you're willing to pay a premium, first class may be a viable option. If you're on a tight budget, standard class on the KTX is still a pleasant and practical option.

Process Of Booking A Ferry

In South Korea, where ferries are a popular mode of transportation, there are several ways to purchase a ferry ticket. Here are a few examples of such approaches:

Online purchasing: Tickets can be purchased in advance on the websites of several ferry companies. Visit the ferry company's website, select the route, dates, and time you want, and then complete the payment process.

Travel agencies: If you're taking a longer trip, booking a ferry ticket through a travel agency is a convenient option. Simply select a travel agency that specializes in South Korean tourism and ask them to arrange for the reservation of your boat ticket.

Directly at the ferry terminal: If you prefer to purchase your ticket in person, you can do so at the ticket counter at the ferry terminal.

By phone: You can purchase your ticket over the phone through the telephone booking services of certain ferry operators. Simply call the ferry operator's customer service number and follow the instructions.

Before purchasing your ferry ticket, double-check the departure and arrival times, the availability of various service classes, and the tariff terms, including any additional taxes or surcharges

Rick Paul

Rick Paul

SEVEN

Final tips and advice for travelers

Congratulations on your decision to visit South Korea! You're in for an unforgettable adventure with so much to see and do. There are a few final tips and pieces of advice to keep in mind as you prepare for your trip to ensure a smooth and enjoyable experience. Read on for some helpful hints on everything from packing essentials to

cultural considerations that will make your trip to South Korea even more enjoyable.

Language and Communication

South Korea's official language is Korean, which is written in the Hangul script. While English is widely spoken in major cities and tourist areas, it is possible that it is less common in more rural areas. It's always useful to know a few basic Korean phrases like "hello" (annyeonghaseyo), "thank you" (gamsahamnida), and "excuse me" (sillyehamnida).

Because public WiFi is not always available, it is best to have a local SIM card or rent a pocket WiFi device for communication. Translation apps can also aid in breaking down language barriers.

Rick Paul

Money and Tipping

South Korea's currency is the Korean won (KRW). Major credit cards such as Visa, Mastercard, and American Express are widely accepted in major cities, but having some cash on hand for smaller transactions or when visiting more rural areas is always a good idea. ATMs are widely available, and many are open around the clock.

Tipping is not common in South Korea because it is included in the bill or service charge. However, tipping is becoming more common in the service industry, particularly for exceptional service.

Health and Safety

South Korea is a relatively safe country to visit, with a low crime rate. However, basic safety precautions, such as keeping an eye on your belongings in crowded areas and being aware of your surroundings, should always be

taken.

South Korea's healthcare system is of high quality, with many modern hospitals and medical facilities. It is recommended that you have travel insurance and bring any necessary medications with you, as some medications may be unavailable.

Local Customs and Etiquette

Respect for elders and hierarchy are highly valued in South Korea. It is customary to use formal titles and honorifics when greeting someone, especially when speaking to someone older or in a position of authority.

When entering homes and some traditional establishments, such as temples and Korean-style restaurants, shoes are typically removed. Blowing your nose in public is also considered impolite.

When dining, it is customary for all dishes to be shared among the group, so it is critical to pick up food with serving utensils rather than your personal chopsticks or spoon. It's also polite to wait for the oldest person to finish their meal before starting your own.

Technology and Connectivity

South Korea has a cutting-edge telecommunications infrastructure that provides fast and dependable internet and cellular service. There is also public WiFi in many places, including airports, cafes, and government buildings.

In addition, many major cities provide free WiFi in public areas such as parks and subway stations. For more dependable and convenient connectivity, visitors can purchase local SIM cards or rent pocket WiFi devices.

South Korea also sells a wide range of electronics and technology, including the most recent smartphones and gadgets.

Future travel considerations

As the world recovers from the COVID-19 pandemic, there are a few things travelers should keep in mind when planning future trips. Here are some important factors to consider:

Destination restrictions: Many countries and regions have implemented international travel restrictions, such as quarantine, health certificates, and vaccination requirements. Before planning a trip, it is critical to research and comprehend these restrictions.

Precautions for health and safety: While vaccination rates continue to rise, it is still critical to take precautions to prevent the spread of COVID-19 and other illnesses.

This may include wearing masks, practicing social distancing, and frequently washing hands.

Travel insurance: With so much uncertainty surrounding travel these days, it is more important than ever to think about purchasing travel insurance. This can cover unexpected flight cancellations, medical emergencies, and other travel-related issues.

As we recover from the pandemic, there is a greater emphasis on sustainable travel practices, such as reducing carbon emissions, supporting local communities, and minimizing environmental impact.

The pandemic has hastened the adoption of technology in the travel industry, from virtual tours and digital check-ins to contactless payment options. Travelers should be ready to use technology to improve their travel experience while minimizing physical contact.

Rick Paul

Travelers can plan and enjoy their future trips with greater confidence and awareness if they keep these considerations in mind.

© Rick Paul

Printed in Great Britain
by Amazon

25226313R00076